NADALADA WAS A NOTHING HEAD

Nadalada was a Nothing Head

TERRY LANCASTER

Copyright © 2025 by Terry Lancaster & The Coalition for Human Kindness All rights reserved. No part of this book may be reproduced in any manner whatsoever without written permission except in the case of brief quotations embodied in critical articles and reviews. First Printing, 2025

Peekaboo. We see you.

All the Flower children

Donned their finest flower hats

And set off on a big adventure

To learn the song of this and that

They climbed the highest mountains

They crossed the deepest seas

They asked philosophers and plowmen

Of what it means to be

The more they lookedy looked

The more there was to find

Until lookedy looky looking

Was all that ever crossed their minds

Hippy McTripperson decided

That enough was just enough

That all the shamans in all the forests

Understood not none of this stuff

So Hippy called a Flower meeting

And all the Flowers came

I'm out said Hippy and left

Without bothering to explain

When Hippy left the Flowers

They were in a far off desert land

With sand in all the places

Where no one really likes sand

That was as good a place as any

To learn about this and that

With all that sand in all those places

The itch becomes the scratch

Hippy needed shelter

Because of course you do

But Hippy had no money

So Hippy slept in a shoe

Now it was a large shoe to begin with

And since Hippy was rather quite small

And since no one else was using it

For no apparent reason at all

All across the desert

Hippy was happy to call it home

Adding a set of shiny wheels

Made it even easier to roam

Pulling the shoe behind

Hippy crossed the sands

Gathering up the necessaries

For dusty desert lands

The first thing you need is water

In the desert you need quite a lot

So Hippy kept a water bag

Filled at every possible spot

One sweltering hot summer day

With the sun so blindingly bright

Hippy was down to the last few drops

With neither spring nor well in sight

As Hippy sat and pondered

Trying to wish up something to drink

From dunes and dunes away

Came the faintest tinkety tink

Hippy climbed the highest dune

Searching for the sound

When the sand suddenly slipped away

And Hippy went tumbling down

Elbow over tea kettle

Hippy kerklumpled through the sand

Landing beside the tiniest tiny bell

In the tiniest tiny hands

Well hello said the tiny stranger

Welcome to our place

May we offer you a cold drink

Perhaps a cool towel for your face?

Aciyagi Kemosabi

Dingity dang dong

The stranger kept ringing the bell

And singing some silly song

Confused and quite befuddled

Hippy took a look around

At the greenest grass you've ever seen

Water just bubbling up from the ground

Yes please I'm so very very thirsty

It's like I haven't drunk in years

I'm so very glad to meet you

So glad I found you here

But you didn't find us said the beller

If that's even what you'd call one

We were never lost to begin with

Only playing peekaboo with the sun

All this water said Hippy

And all this happy green grass

Where on Earth did it come from?

How much longer can it last?

Hippy gazed in wide wonder

As they wandered across the sand

Grass and water and stranger

Walking as if hand in hand

Wherever we go said the stranger

We're already where we are

The water and grass are always there

Like the sun the moon the stars

You can only see them of course

When they're all lined up just right

Looking for water in the desert

Is like looking for the sun at night

The harder that you look

The harder it is to find

We quit looking for water long ago

The thirst itself will ruin your mind

I'm always looking for water said Hippy

Everywhere I go

I find the highest sand dune

And look around real nice and slow

I've climbed every dune in the desert

Circled all four corners once and again

There's no water to be found anywhere

Nothing here but sand and wind

The tiny stranger with the tiny bell laughed

Oh that just gives us the wiggles

It's the funniest thing we've ever heard

Shimmying and shaking between the giggles

Looking for water on top of a mountain

That just sounds downright silly

Birds and bees and thirsty trees know

That water flows down hilly

When you're thirsty be water

You gotta follow the Flow

In the hollow between the rivers

There's water everywhere we go

And on that confusing note

Stranger and oasis wandered away

Leaving only sand and Hippy

Wait wait wait can't you stay?

We could just hang out here

That'd be kind of groovy

Or maybe I could come with

I'm born to move me

The Flowers and me we roamed all over

And we learned a great big lot

But there's some tiny bit of something

That we never just quite got

I've got so much more to learn

And you probably know a thing or two

I don't even know your name

Or even what you do

We are no one said the stranger

We have no tales to tell

Then the stranger wandered away

Dingity ding dinging on the bell

In a world of all the sad sad scenes

That Hippy McTripperson had ever sadly sadly seen

That was the saddest sadly seeing

Hippy had ever even dreamed

In all of the excitement

Just seeing all that H 2 O

Hippy had simply forgotten

To get one single drop to go

Looking at the empty water bag

As the stranger disappeared from sight

Hippy sank head into hands in the sand

Overwhelmed by this thirsty plight

As the sun reached its zenith

Hippy sank deeper and deeper

Deep into the sandy sand

Into the sleepiest sleepy sleeper

Maybe it was all just a mirage

Maybe there never was a stranger

Maybe it was just a fevered dream

To keep Hippy's mind off the danger

All through the long hot day

The sun raced across the sky

The moon chasing behind

As the cold dark night went by

Hippy dreamed of rivers

Flowing side by side

Flowing into the ocean

Stretching far and wide

Where one river ended

And the other river began

There was no separation

There was no line in the sand

IN THE SAND! screamed Hippy

Just as the sun began to rise

Hippy was neck-deep in sand

And that was quite the surprise

A surprise too the water

Which in the divots nearby had pooled

When the dew formed around Hippy

As the moonlit desert cooled

Hippy gathered the water

One drippity drop at a time

Soon the water bag was filled to the top

Which greatly eased Hippy's mind

With the water situation settled

And provisions well in hand

Hippy literally had had it up to here

With this unpleasant desert land

With mountain peaks and shaman sheiks

And everyone trying to explain

Why their explanation was explainier

Than any every other Tom Dick & Jane's

Whatever we set our sights on

Whatever we're looking for

It's always just over the hill

Not quite yet or maybe just before

I'm off the road said Hippy

Away back home I go

The way of course was obvious

Just simply follow the Flow

Down the road went Hippy

Getting by and getting along

Putting one foot in front of the other

Whistling a little song

Sleeping at day

Traveling at night

Following the Flow

Hippy did alright

The water bag stayed mostly full

Sometimes more than others

And the food for Hippy's belly

Wasn't always Hippy's druthers

But it kept Hippy moving

Or at least flowing downhill

Until one night around sunrise

Hippy took a terrible spill

Hippy's shoe hit a pothole

Bigger than Hippy had ever seen

It tore the wheels right off

Hippy's shoe-shaped roaming machine

With no way to fix the axle

With no way to move the shoe

Hippy looked around for a place to sleep

Any sliver of shade would do

With the morning sun still rising

Hippy caught a glint in the sands

Oceans and oceans of water

Where sand and sea join hands

From the desert came a familiar tune

But a not so familiar sound

Rumbling deep and low

Footsteps shaking the ground

The giant was way way taller than Hippy

Wider and faster too

Hippy got pretty scared

And didn't know what to do

As the giant rumbled by

Bells ring a ding-dinging

Hippy suddenly recognized the song

The lofty stranger was singing

Aciyagi Kemosabi

Jijimuguy

Bodi soho bodi soho

Aciyagi aciyi

The words meant nothing to Hippy

Just gibberish and gobbledygooky

The tune was exactly the same though

And Hippy found that quite spooky

It was the song from the desert mirage

The song of the tiny stranger

And this giant in front of Hippy

Suddenly seemed less a danger

Whoa hold up stretch let me holler at ya

Hippy shouted chasing after the giant

I dig that tune you're singing

Teach me the words so I can try it?

The words don't really matter said the giant

That's not how you'll understand

Our ship is sailing presently though

We're leaving behind this land

What a coinky dinky said Hippy

That's where I want to go

You think maybe I can catch a ride?

I'm just following the Flow

As you wish said the giant

Go ahead and hop on

We must get to the shore and quick

Our ship will soon be gone

It didn't take much time at all

With the giant's long long strides

But the ship was already sailing away

Before Hippy's tall friend arrived

One step into the water

Another splash into the depths

Hippy and the tall tall stranger

Climbed aboard and caught their breaths

Jijimuguy there was written

Across the back of the ship

As sandy shore drifted away

As surly bonds did slip

Out upon the ocean blue

Hippy was now set sail

Following the Flow the winds the currents

Freed from sandy shores' jail

After all that time in the desert

This was quite a place to be

Hippy was now surrounded by water

As far as the eye could see

Water water everywhere thought Hippy

But not a drop to drink

And this ship doesn't look all that sturdy

What if we start to sink?

There was no shore to swim to

No safe harbor awaiting arrival

Hippy became deeply concerned

About their chances for survival

Where are we going anyway?

When are we going to arrive?

Do we have enough of the necessaries?

To make such a trip alive?

We're already here said the giant

Who wasn't really quite so big

Now quietly crossing the deck

Humming and dancing that jig

It's actually a pleasant trip

Just sit back and enjoy the ride

Watch the waves rise and fall

Feel the ship roll side to side

If you always wonder where you're going

You'll hardly notice when you get there

Feel the sun on your skin breathe it all in

Cool crisp salty sea air

Quit trying to be somewhere else

Just be wherever you are

Right here right now

Make this moment your North Star

Home is where your feets is

No map could ever compare

To opening your eyes and looking around

Go ahead if you dare

Whoa hold up now said Hippy

I'm all for going with the Flow

But if nobody knows where we're going

How do we know which way to go?

You're saying the captain hasn't charted the stars

That no one is watching the tides?

What about storms and such?

Just how big a wave can we ride?

That's a good one laughed the stranger

Dancing while standing still

There's no captain on this ship

No one's up there spinning the wheel

The waves are gonna take us

Where the waves are gonna go

Just how big a wave we can ride

There's only one way to know

Big storms are gonna come

That's just the way it be

The trick to riding the storm out

Is leaning into the waves with glee

With that the not so giant giant

Leapt out into the ocean

Paddling behind a single board

As thunder commenced commotion

Oh it's gonna be a big one said the stranger

Gonna be quite the show

We're so very excited for you

Good luck and off you go

What do you mean good luck screamed Hippy

What am I supposed to do now?

How do I steer this ship anyway?

Where are you going anyhow?

You can't just leave me here like this

What's your name so I can leave a review?

I'm gonna let people know

What an awful guide are you

If I make it through this that is

But I haven't got a chance

I am going to drown here in this ocean

Sighed Hippy as waves began their dance

☺

Who are you trying to save asked the stranger

You think you're the story's star?

How can you drown in the ocean?

When ocean is all you are?

We have no name to speak of

A name is definitely what we're not

We're no particular wave in the ocean

We're the ocean within a drop

We are sorrow and sickness

We are suffering and pain

We are joy and redemption

The sunshine and the rain

We are the storm that you're afraid of

We are the salvation that you seek

We are everything and nothing

Open your eyes and take a peak

We are no one said the stranger

Surfing away on the ship's name platte

Jijimuguy was all it said

There is no this and that

☺

No one again scoffed Hippy

Every which way I turn

Everybody's claiming to be nobody

Like it's some lesson to learn

Not a lot of nothing

That's what I have to say

Filling my head with nonsense

On such a terrible day

Bad things are about to happen

The situation is dire and getting worse

I'm going to my watery grave

Without the secrets of the universe

Hippy climbed the tallest mast

As the wind about did scream

Looking for any signs of land

Wishing it were all a dream

There was no land to mention

No hint of distant shore

And Hippy saw what's left to see

When nothing's left to look for

That's when it started raining

Only a little at first

Then much harder and faster

Going from bad to worse

Lightning flashed and thunder rolled

The waves grew taller and taller

Hippy's hopes for survival

Grew quickly smaller and smaller

The sky was black as midnight

Then so suddenly bright

That Hippy started to laugh

Despite the terrible plight

On again and off again

Round and round it goes

If it ain't one thing it's another

That's all anybody knows

Over the roar of the storm

So quietly Hippy could hardly tell

Way way off in the distance

No One dinging the bell

Suddenly Hippy was in the water

The boat just simply wasn't there

Hippy was hanging on for dear life

When it just vanished into thin air

The sea itself was blank and black

So too the clouds and sky

The rain poured like a river

With no patch of air left dry

Sky and ocean joined together

No horizon to be found

Nothing there but ocean

360 degrees around

Or was it 360 degrees of rain-drenched sky?

There was really no way to tell

Through whatever the heck it was

Hippy fell

With nothing to grab onto

Nothing to see or show

Hippy realized this was home

And at long last let go

The roar of ocean and thunder

Louder than loud can be

Still boom boom booming

Only now almost quietly

Falling through the blackness

As night turned into day

With nothing to measure against though

How far was the fall is impossible to say

Through an uncarved block of ocean and sky

There was nothing but the fall

What had seemed a great big something

Was really no thing at all

Falling with style or flying

Floating in empty sky

It's all the same when there are no names

Only rejoicing with no need for why

Tumbling stumbling and rolling

Riding the waves and wind

Letting go and joining the game

With no start middle or end

Into the void went Hippy

Nothing to see hear touch or smell

Emptiness from all four corners

The bottom of a deep dark well

Hippy couldn't see a single thing

Not fingers knees nor toes

But everything still felt connected

As plain as the face on Hippy's nose

When the toes began to wiggle

Way off yonder in the dark

Hippy could feel the wiggling

Like a tiny little spark

In and out and in and out

As Hippy breathed deep deep breaths

The spark followed all about

Rising and falling with lungs and chest

I'm breathing thought Hippy

Although I don't know how

Breathing in the ocean

That I'm a different part of now

The spark that Hippy thought was Hippy

Was something of a different kind

You tend to think your mind's inside your head

But your head's all in your mind

Maybe spark isn't even the right word

Maybe more like a little twitch

Maybe something you just wanna scratch

Whenever it starts to itch

From the tippy top of Hippy's head

To Hippy's trippy toes

That little bit of something

Just grows and grows and grows

Hippy could almost see it now

Flowing like a river

Moving one part of Hippy to another

One part taker one part giver

Connecting all the pieces and parts

That Hippy had always called me

Never giving a moments thought

To what they truly be

But fingers and toes aren't the beginning

Eyes and ears aren't the end

Honestly you can't even tell

Where ocean stops and Hippy begins

The spark becomes a river

The river becomes a sea

Hippy becomes the ocean

Just like you and me

For a while Hippy is whale food

In the belly of the beast

For a while Hippy is plant food

When the whale poops out the feast

The spark grows into sunshine

That fills the ocean floor

Until sea and sky become one again

The same as they were before

Hippy is connected to it all it seems

That's the way it's always been

Hippy is every thing all at once

Hippy is no thing in the end

There's no such thing as a thing you see

Everything's a part of something else

There's no way that any thing could ever be

A thing all by itself

Thoughts are just things that haven't thinged yet

Emotions a phantasmagorical zoo

Which leads to the obvious question then

Just who the heck are you?

The thinker of thoughts is only a thought

A thought that's never been

Anything more and nothing less

Than a passing fancy's whim

A big box of nothing it is

with nothing inside to see

you can look 6 ways to Sunday

and nothing will ever be

All in all it's nothing at all

A tapestry of thread and stitcher

A fart in the wind a gambler's spin

The which than which no which is whicher

Nadalada was a Nothing Head now

Awakened on that far shore

Whatever it was that Hippy was

Hippy was no more

At the bottom of the Hollow

Where the river runs deep and wide

Nadalada sat so very still

So very glad to be alive

There's nowhere to go said Nadalada

There's no place else to see

It's all right here right now

So this is where we'll be

With no other thoughts in Nadalada's head

With no passing flights of fancy

Nadalada simply sat there

And never not once got antsy

It could have been a thousand lifetimes

Maybe just a moment or three

But for that eternal moment

Nadalada was completely free

Then Nadalada got hungry

A little cold and thirsty too

After all that time in the ocean

Fresh river water would nicely do

Nadalada drank from the river

Then gathered wood for the fire

With no axe to do the chopping

Only the tiniest sticks were required

Rubbing sticks together

For a quite extensive time

Nadalada thought of rubbing sticks

With only that in mind

A spark of light a wisp of smoke

A tiny glowing ember

Nadalada fanned the flames

Then went off in search of dinner

Picking mussels from the river

Picking berries from the shore

Nadalada was ever thankful

Wishing for nothing more

Whistling a happy tune

Doing a happy dance

Nadalada prepared the evening meal

From hap and happenstance

Everything Nadalada needed

Was where it was supposed to be

And when the evening meal was finished

Nadalada slept beneath the giant chestnut tree

Dreaming again of twin rivers

Flowing from mountains high

Water clear as glass

Falling gently from the sky

Clouds like floating lakes

Bursting at the seams

The Flow filled heavens and earth

In Nadalada's dreams

Nadalada watched it all unfold

Like a movie or play

Like a never-ending story

With each a part to play

Soaring high above

In the bluest part of the sky

The blackest of all black dots

Barely visible to the eye

As the dot got closer and closer

It almost looked like a bird

With talons and beak glistening

Like a steely razor-sharp sword

The dream it seemed had ended

The dot it seemed a raptor

Nadalada seemed somewhat tasty

Morning's breakfast to be after

After being eaten by a whale

Much to Nadalada's chagrin

Nadalada was in no big hurry

To ever do that again

Everybody's gotta eat said Nadalada

It wasn't a matter of being afraid

It was only to keep the game afoot

That Nadalada jumped up to say

Wake up wake up

In a voice so strong and true

The hungry hawk simply forgot how to fly

Forgot which trick to do

The hawk landed gently by Nadalada

All hunger now satisfied

Filled with awareness and joy

Of simply being alive

Wake up said Nadalada

We've found our way home

We've found this Happy Hollow

With no more trails to roam

No more seeking no more chasing

No more getting lost in the maze

In Happy Hollow we abide in kindness

Rejoicing in each day

We can have everything we want

If we want no thing at all

Wake up from the dream of desire

Wake up one and all

Wake up cried the hawk

Taking to the sky

Wake up wake up

Its joyful battle cry

The hawk sailed away

As Nadalada settled in

Building a life in Happy Hollow

Starting from naught again

A little hut on the hillside

Built from twigs and leaves

A little patch of taters

Growing near the trees

A couple of handfuls of carrot tops

Blowing in the wind

Fishes and mussels galore

When the rains came and went

Nothing much to brag about

Nothing much to see

At home in Happy Hollow

Nadalada could simply be

And so it went for Nadalada

One day the same as the next

Each one completely different

In a completely different respect

Winters come and summers go

The grass grows taller than tall

The rivers ebb and rise

Nadalada watches it all

Rejoicing in the way things are

Dancing and singing the song

Nothing at all to worry about

Nothing could ever be wrong

With all that singing and shouting in the Hollow

Word began to spread

Eventually the neighbors started to wonder

About Nadalada the Nothing Head

What's that weirdo doing down there?

Maybe we should have a talk

Maybe teach this Nadalada a thing or two

About how to walk the walk

Some came down to argue

Some came down to fight

Others came down to scoff

At Nadalada's ridiculous plight

Living in a makeshift hut

At the bottom of a hill

Why I never they all laughed

And I guess I never will

Many came looking for riches

For land and mineral fees

For fish and fur and feathers

For giant chestnut trees

Some sought to save Nadalada

And Nadalada's eternal soul

Preaching of a kingdom hereafter

But mostly looking for gold

A few were looking for answers

Answers they hadn't found

To questions about life in Pumpkin Ridge

And other nearby towns

And lastly some came mostly

Because they had nowhere else

No family no friends no nothing

Lost and in search of themselves

Many came and many went

Nadalada watched them come and go

Very few ever stuck around

Abiding in Happy Hollow

The ones that stayed found something

They were never looking for

The ones that left still seeking

The same as they were before

Maybe a dozen Nothing Heads

In a handful of hillside huts

In a land down by the river

Eating berries and nuts

Singing and dancing and being still

Watching the flowers grow

The Nothing Heads were going nowhere

With no particular place to go

Aciyagi Kemosabi

Jijimuguy

Bodi soho bodi soho

Aciyagi aciyi

The Nothing Heads sang together

As the stones of truth they lay

In the deep dark scary woods

Near Happy Hollow's hidden way

It wasn't really a warning

It wasn't exactly a map

Just a casual observation

A simple statement of fact

Seek not the Kingdom

Nadalada carved in letters bold

Seek not the Treasure

From tales long foretold

Seek not the answers

To questions large and small

Those who enter Happy Hollow

Shall seek no thing at all

The End

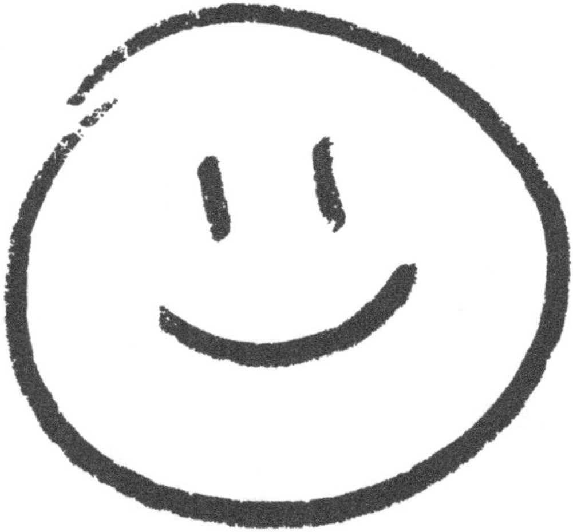

Written by **Terry Lancaster**

Published by
The Coalition for Human Kindness

Abiding in kindness for ourselves
and the world in which we live

BeKindClub.org

Also available from
The Coalition for Human Kindness

Here Come The Nothing Heads

If Dr. Seuss, the Dalai Lama, and Jeffrey "The Dude" Lebowski walked into a bar **Here Come The Nothing Heads** is what you might get.

An epic poem for children of all ages, Here Come The Nothing Heads tells the tale of Sneezy McSneezerson, Grouchy McGroucherson, and Fluffy McFlufferson who live in the fanciest pumpkin high atop Pumpkin Ridge, but they are banished by town Elders because they can't get along with each other or anyone else.

They must travel to Happy Hollow, home of the mysterious tribe of Nothing Heads, and learn how to live in peace. The trials and tribulations of their adventure force them to look at life in a brand new way that was as old as time itself.

BeKindClub.org

The Coalition for Human Kindness publishes books, audiobooks, and videos - available on our website and at some of the coolest bookstores, gift shops, and roadside fortune-teller stands ever (Amazon & Audible too).

When you **join the Coalition**, you get free access to all of our titles in digital and audio formats, free Be Kind Club apparel, and wholesale pricing on printed books. We're fans of seeing the big wide world do as the big wide world likes to do. Here are a handful of our favorite places to sit and watch. **Your membership helps us support them. Thanks.**

Friends of Land Between the Lakes
Friends of Cross Creek National Wildlife Refuge
Friends of Harpeth River State Park
Friends of Shelby Park & Bottoms
Big South Fork National River & Recreation Area
Dr. Julian G. Bruce St. George Island State Park

BeKindClub.org

www.ingramcontent.com/pod-product-compliance
Lightning Source LLC
LaVergne TN
LVHW040422160425
808755LV00002B/19